Joyce's Gems
"Joyce Meyer Quotes"

Encouraging Words
Of
Faith, Hope
And
Instant Inspiration

By Don Pasco

http://www.EbooksWorthReading.com

Joyce Meyer's website can be found here:
https://www.joycemeyer.org/

Other books by Don Pasco

JOEL'S GEMS

"Joel Osteen Jokes"

Happy As a Rat In a Trash Can

How to Raise Your Happiness Level

ISBN-13: 978-1511423953
ISBN-10: 1511423951

Table of Contents

INTRODUCTION

Many years ago when I first came across Joyce Meyer on a television broadcast she immediately caught my attention. She reminded me of my Grandmother (though the years between us are not that many), but it didn't take long to feel a connection with her. She spoke very directly and didn't mince any words. I like that and I'm sure Granny would have liked that too (she's no longer with us, R.I.P.).

I'm one of those people that you probably don't want to watch TV with because my attention span is short and I'm quicker on the draw with my remote control then Wyatt Earp was with his .45 revolver. So, the fact that Joyce held my attention long enough to keep the channel on until the end of the show says something about her charismatic personality and teaching style.

Although I often watch many different "speakers" (for lack of a better term) on the Trinity Broadcast Network (TBN), they don't all speak to my heart... and once I've made that determination you're either "in" or "out" for all future passes up (or down) the channel listings. In case you didn't figure it out already, Joyce is "in" and I have never been disappointed with her messages.

Inside this book, I have compiled an excellent collection of Joyce Meyer quotes and if you too are a fan, I'm quite sure you will appreciate many of these quotes that have inspired me and will more than likely inspire you.

The thing I love about quotes is they say so much in just a few sentences and often times in a single sentence.

I'm not sure if this would qualify as a quote or not... many have referred to it as a motto or slogan, but back in the early 1900's, it has been said that Mr. Thomas J. Watson (the chairman of IBM), positively affected the entire organization by having the word "THINK" placed in offices, plants and company publications. During Watson's first four years as president, revenues more than doubled. Hopefully you agree that words (and quotes) can be very powerful.

I hope that you will find a few "gems" here that you will hold dear to help you with your challenges going forward. You may even want to memorize your favorites. You never know when a situation might arise to help someone else or share them on facebook. Just don't forget to give Joyce the credit.

Let's get started!

HOW GOD SEES YOU

"God loves you constantly!
You belong to God.
In His eyes you have
infinite worth and value.
If you have been rejected or treated badly,
don't let resentment build up in your heart.
Keep your eyes on God
and follow His instructions.
Always believe what God says about you
above your own feelings
or what others say about you.
God's opinion is the only one that matters."

****

"You are a miracle waiting to happen."

****

"God is not surprised
by your inabilities, your imperfections,
or your faults.
He has always known everything about you,
things you are just now finding out,
and He chose you on purpose for Himself."

****

"God is not surprised.
"We often act as though God is shocked
to discover that we fail or make mistakes.
The truth is: God has a big eraser,
and He uses it
to keep our records clean and clear."

****

"You can have a wonderful, amazing,
awesome life just like anybody else.
You just need to see yourself
the way God sees you."

****

"God loves you as much at this moment
as He ever will in your whole life.

No amount of anything you do
is going to make God love you
any more or less."

New York Times Bestseller

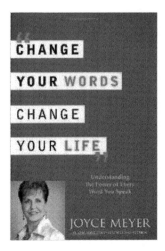

PRAYER

A Prayer Against Depression: God, I have been carrying a heavy burden and I am coming to You right now for relief. I surrender all my hurts, disappointments and insecurities to You. Thank You for Your Word, which tells me about Your unconditional love and affection for me. You are my Father, and I am Your child. I love to be in Your presence, You are the source of all my peace and joy. Forever I will praise You. Amen.

****

A Prayer to Help You Forgive: I ask for Your healing hand to touch me and for Your unconditional love to flood my heart so I can forgive [name a specific person] as quickly and as thoroughly as You have forgiven me. Lord, I release my offense to You right now. Thank You for forgiving me of my sins, and for using me today to reflect the perfect love of Your Son and my Savior, Jesus Christ. Amen

****

A Prayer for God's Help: God, I need your help. I'm really struggling with [say what's on your heart] and I know I can't figure out a solution on my own. I pray that You will show me what to do. I'm listening, Lord. Help me remember that I'm not alone. You've got me in the palm of Your hand and that's the best place to be. Amen.

****

A Prayer for Greater Faith: God, it isn't always easy to believe You're in heaven, hearing my prayers. Sometimes it sounds too good to be true. But Your Word says, You will never leave me or forsake me. You're sticking with me. And I want to stick with You. Lord, help me to use the faith You've already given me to stand in faith for [say what's on your heart]. I know that whatever Your will for my life will come to pass if I keep going forward and trusting You to do what I can't do. Nothing is impossible for You, Lord. And I choose to trust in You. Amen.

****

"Prayer is simply conversation with God.
It doesn't need to be long, loud or fancy.
What's important is
the sincerity of our heart
and the confidence
that God hears and will answer us.

****

We must develop the confidence
that even if we simply say,
"God help me,"
He hears and will answer."
****

"Don't just pray for God to open doors,
pray for God to close doors in your life that
need to be closed."
****

"Don't wait to pray.
Pray right away and don't delay."
****

"If you will make time with God
your first priority,
everything else in your life
will fall into place."
****

FORGIVENESS

"If forgiveness were a drug,
it would be considered a miracle cure
because of all the amazing things
it does for us."

****

"The Bible tells us we're blessed
when we forgive.
No matter how hard it is, forgive.
There's nothing more painful than
living with your heart full of hate.
Don't sink to the enemy's level.
Choose today to release yourself
from the yoke of bitterness
and start enjoying life."

****

"We all have weaknesses,
but God is a God of redemption
and He's always there to lift us out
of any pit that we have gotten into."

****

"Forgive your enemies quickly.
Your anger won't change them
so why be miserable all day.
GOD IS YOUR VINDICATOR!"

****

"Be kind, don't judge and criticize,
forgive quickly, and be merciful."

****

"Don't let the way other people treat you
determine your wealth and value."

****

"We desperately want people
to believe we are okay...
to think we've got it together.
But it's okay to not be okay."

****

"It may not be easy to forgive people
that have hurt you
but it's much easier
than staying bitter all your life."

****

TRUST IN THE LORD

"Have you ever tried to solve a problem
only God can solve?
The more we try to make our own way,
the tighter the doors stay closed.
But when we do things God's way,
He can open doors for us suddenly."

****

"We should trust God's love
even when we cannot discern His purpose."

****

"Victory in the present
requires you
to move past the past."

****

"If you need to take medicine, take it.
If you need to go to the doctor, go.

But don't do anything without trusting God
to bring healing in your life
because even when medicine can't do it,
even when man can't do it,
God can still heal you.
He is still a miracle-working God!"

****

"Before you can get up on the outside,
you must get up on the inside."

****

"You can't trust God to give you
everything you want,
but you can trust God to give you
the very best that He has for you."

****

"It's time to give God the hurts
of your past and let Him give you

the healing and restoration
you're longing for."

****

"Choose to hear the voice of God
and to think about the things He says,
not the things the enemy says."

****

NEW BEGINNINGS

Aren't you glad our God
is the God of second chances?

****

"It's never too late for you to begin again,
but don't think for one minute
that when you step out to try
that the enemy won't take
a step against you
to try to drive you back."

****

"A new beginning is not an elevator ride.
And it's not an escalator ride.
It's a walk of faith, one step at a time."

****

"If you're living with pain or
disappointment,
maybe you feel like you've hit
a roadblock in your life,
it's never too late for your fresh start.
You can begin again."

****

"With God,
new beginnings aren't the exception;
they're the rule."

****

"Don't ever stop dreaming,
no matter how old you are.
Even if you've had some
shattered dreams in your life,
I want to encourage you to dream again."

****

"Instead of giving up, get up and press
into the new beginning
that God has for you,

and live the life
that God wants you to live."

****

"No matter what you have done,
God is not turning his face away from you.
God is looking toward you and
He's reaching His hands out to you
right now.
And it's not too late for you to have
a fresh start."

****

"Time after time, story after story,
page after page God offers a new beginning.
The circumstances change,
and the stories vary,
but the grace of God never wavers."

****

"Small beginnings are miracles
in seed form."

****

DISCIPLINE,

SELF-CONTROL & OBEDIENCE

"We are free to make our own choices,
but we are not free
from the consequences of our choices."

****

"Whatever your goals are,
there's one thing for certain —
it will be almost impossible to get there
without discipline and self-control."

****

"You'd be surprised at what God can do
when you are obedient with just one step."

****

"You can't control
what thoughts enter your head,
but you can decide
if they'll stay there."

****

Prayer for Obedience:

"Thank You for leading me, God.
I pray that Your strength and wisdom
would be with me as I make decisions
that follow Your path.
Help me to put Your Word
to the test in my life
so that my obedience will be a blessing
to everyone who sees You working in me.
Lord, help me to stay focused on You
so the obstacles that come up
won't seem impossible to overcome.
I know all things are possible through You,
and I thank You for the privilege
of doing any small task
that brings You glory.

Let my name be forgotten, Lord,
and Yours be remembered. Amen."

****

"Just be yourself.
Don't find someone who seems
to have it all together
and then try your best
to be like they are.
Be the best "you"
that you can be!"

****

"Power is connected to obedience.
We don't buy power with our obedience,
but I believe that when we're obedient
it proves that we're mature enough
for God to release that power
and that anointing in our life."

****

BLESSING OTHERS

"If you want to increase your joy today,
do something for another person
that increases theirs."

****

"I will be kind and show mercy.
Humility is the attitude
of the heart and mind
that God requires of us.
Never, under any circumstances,
are we to view ourselves
as better than others.
Give God what He truly requires,
which is to do what is just,
love mercy and kindness,
and walk humbly with Him."

****

"The best thing that we can do
when we have problems
is to help somebody else with a need.
I believe it releases something in us
that's beautiful,
and it also releases the power of God
to go to work in our life
like never before."

****

"When you feel down,
go be a blessing to somebody else."

****

"I don't believe anything puts a bigger smile
on God's face than when we
help little children,
because they really are helpless
without someone that will help them."

****

"When we reach out to other people,
it takes our minds off of ourselves,

which is one of the best things
that can happen to us,
and then as we reach out to other people,
a life begins to flow through us
that is the life of Christ
that we experienced
when He gave Himself to us."

****

"Something beautiful opens up in us
when we open up our hearts
and we want to make
somebody else's life better."

****

WHAT GOD WANTS

"We are not anointed by God to give up.
We're anointed by God
to press in and press on
And be the people God wants us to be,
do what He wants us to do
and have what He wants us to have."

****

"God wants us to rest,
but He doesn't want us to rust!
Are you getting enough exercise
to stay healthy?"

****

"I actually believe God wants us
to grow spiritually

to the point where we are
more concerned about what people
are doing to themselves
when they hurt us
than what they're actually doing to us."

****

"Don't let fear stop you from stepping out
and being all that God wants you to be."

****

"God wants to do more for us
than just keep us out of Hell.
He wants us to live fulfilling lives
of love and service in Him."

****

"Don't be satisfied with some kind of
a mediocre okay, barely-get-along life.
Go for the very best life
that God has for you."

****

"God wants you to
enjoy your life now,
not when."

****

JOY

"Don't postpone being glad
until everything is perfect –
be glad today!"

****

"Joy is our strength and actually
energizes us,
so I encourage you to take every
opportunity you have
to smile and laugh!"

****

"Don't waste today regretting the past
or dreading the future.
Enjoy this day
because it is a gift from God!"

****

"Your "too late" is God's "just in time.""

****

"Not only has your past been paid for,
your future has been provided for."

****

"You can overcome every obstacle,
as long as you refuse to give up,
because you have the Spirit of God
inside of you."

****

"The hungrier you are for God,
the happier you're going to be."

****

"To be able to enjoy life
and avoid unnecessary problems,
you and I must live
according to the truth
in God's Word

and not according to the lies we hear from other people, the world, or the enemy."

****

"A Good Attitude Doesn't Come From
Having the Best of Everything in life;
It Comes from Making
the Best of Everything in Life!"

****

"No matter what has happened to you
in your life,
you don't have to have a bad attitude
if you don't want to."

****

FAITH

"All things with God are possible,
but not all things with God
are positively going to happen
while we just sit back & do nothing."

****

"Ask for and expect God's favor today
and every day.
God can open doors for you
that no man can open."

****

"When you are in a storm,
remember that the rough weather
won't last forever!!"

****

"If you don't give up on your faith
and you hold fast to your faith,
it will bring results."

****

"You don't have to have
some special feeling to believe.
You can just choose to believe the Truth
that Jesus died for all your sins
over 2,000 years ago
and He loves you."

****

"What you don't understand now,
you will understand later.
We live life forward.
We understand it backward."

****

"Just because you can't see it yet,
doesn't mean it's not on its way."

****

"Regret is a power drainer.
"I wish I wouldn't have.
I wish I would have."
Well, if you didn't you didn't,
and if you did you did.
So this is today and let's be now people
because faith is now."

****

"The answer to your problem
is not worry,
but praying and trusting
that Jesus is leading you."

****

"God has got a good plan for you,
and there's nothing in your past
that can prevent you
from having a good life,
if you will really learn how to believe
what God says about you."

****

GOD'S LOVE

"None of us could ever be good enough
to deserve anything that God does for us.
But that doesn't need
to make us feel down about ourselves;
it needs to make us amazed
at God's goodness."

****

"There is nothing you've done wrong
that is too big for God to fix.
He can truly make all things
work together for good,
not only for you
but for your children too."

****

"We don't have it all together
and we are imperfect,
but we are the ones
that Jesus died for."

****

"God doesn't want us to have
broken hearts, wounded emotions
and messed up personalities.

He wants us to know who we are in Christ
and to receive His unconditional love."

****

"When God gives you a desire
for something,
He will give you peace along with it."

****

"As a believer in Jesus Christ,
you are His child.
You may not always act
the way He wants you to,

but you never stop being His child.

God will never give up on us!"

****

HOW TO PLEASE GOD

"Don't ever run at your giants
with your mouth shut.
You need to run at 'em saying,
"I know who I am
and I know who I belong to.
I am a child of the living God."

****

"What enables you to do anything
that you need to do in life?
It's knowing the Word
and speaking the Word,
especially when
your circumstances stink."

****

"The best way to interrupt a bad thought
is by saying something positive."

****

"To delight yourself in the Lord
and let Him give you the desires
of your heart is much better
than struggling
while trying to get things for yourself."

****

"Dig in with both heels and say,
"I am never going to quit
and I am never going to give up.
Devil, you just go wear yourself out
bothering somebody else
because I am going to get
from the pit to the palace
and you are not going to stop me."

****

"Pleasing God is not nearly as hard
as you may think.

Simple, childlike faith pleases Him."

****

"Anytime that we're willing
to do what's right
and we depend on God,
His grace is activated in our life
and He enables us to do it."

****

"Even though you're not
where you need to be,
thank God you're not
where you used to be.
You're making the journey,
and you're not going to quit
until you arrive."

****

MISCELLANEOUS

"Truth is not relative to the age we live in.
Truth is truth and it doesn't change."

****

"Your history doesn't have to be your
destiny."

****

"God can do more in one moment
than you can do in a lifetime."

****

"Some of you right now
are in the wilderness of your life
and whether you know it or not,
He's working some junk out of you

---

that needs to come out
before you're going to be ready
to have what God has promised you."

****

"Everybody's always looking for a word,
here's a word: LOVE
Walk in love,
that will keep you busy
for the rest of your life."

****

"The most important moment in your life
is this moment right now
because it's the only one
that you know for sure that you have."

****

The End

IF YOU ENJOYED THIS BOOK PLEASE TELL
YOUR FRIENDS ABOUT IT

Other books by Don Pasco

Joel Osteen Quotes

Joel Osteen Jokes

Happy as a Rat in a Trash Can

**Name That Artist – The Multiple Choice Music
Celebrity Quiz Game**

**Name That Band – The Multiple Choice Music
Quiz Game**

Recommended Reads

You Can Begin Again:
No Matter What, It's Never Too Late
By Joyce Meyer

The Approval Fix:
How to Break Free from People Pleasing
By Joyce Meyer

The 7 Most Powerful Prayers
That Will Change Your Life Forever!
By Adam Houge

Happy As a Rat In a Trash Can
How to Raise Your Happiness Level
By Don Pasco

Break Out!
5 Keys to Go Beyond Your Barriers
and Live an Extraordinary Life
By Joel Osteen

One Last Thing

Thank you for taking the time to read
Joyce Meyer Quotes.

If you enjoyed this book or found it useful I'd be very grateful if you'd post a short review on Amazon. Your support really does make a difference and I read all the reviews personally so I can get your feedback and make this book even better.

If you'd like to leave a review just go to Don's Author page here:

https://www.ebooksworthreading.com
And look for this title.

Don Pasco's Websites
http://DonPasco.com
http://BestJoelOsteenQuotes.com
Don Pasco's Facebook Fan Pages
http://facebook.com/DonPascoBooks
http://facebook.com/BestJoelOsteenQuotes

For more information about Joyce Meyer

and Joyce Meyer Ministries

Please visit:

https://www.joycemeyer.org/

https://www.facebook.com/joycemeyerministries

Unadvertised Bonus

Here is an EXCERPT from Don's "Happy As a Rat In a Trash Can"

HAPPY AS A RAT IN A TRASH CAN

How to Raise Your Happiness Level

By Don Pasco

http://donpasco.com

http://www.EbooksWorthReading.com

INTRODUCTION

Only 1 life that soon will pass…
Only what's done with love will last

Many years ago I saw a drawing of an elephant with 5 men who were all blindfolded. Each of the blindfolded men were experiencing the elephant in a different way.

- One was sitting on top of it.
- Another was holding the elephant's tail.
- One was holding the elephant's trunk
- while another was hugging the elephant's leg,
- And the 5th was grasping the elephant's ear.

I don't recall whether or not there was a caption that went along with the drawing, but I was strongly impacted by the message it conveyed. It was obvious that each of those men, if asked to describe the elephant, would have completely different opinions.

That drawing still sticks in my mind today and reminds me that we all see things differently, even though we may be experiencing the exact same thing.

If you will let this image impact you the way it did me, you can become a more understanding person of people and situations in *your* life. You can become a little more tolerant of things you don't understand, because you will know that there is always more to every situation than meets the eye.

Our Senses Are Limited

Also, it's important to realize that as wonderful as it is to have our 5 senses, they are limited.

Just for example purposes, let's talk about our hearing. Most of us know that dogs and cats can hear things that we humans cannot.

According to Wikipedia:

The range of human hearing is typically considered to be between 20 Hz and 18 kHz.

The top end of a dog's hearing range is about 45 kHz, while a cat's is 64 kHz

http://en.wikipedia.org/wiki/Dog_whistle

Keep this thought in mind when we get to the section on faith.

Perhaps it is why the bible tells us to:

"walk by faith; not by sight."
2 Corinthians 5:7

Happiness –
A Universal Desire

What is happiness and why do we want it?

According to dictionary.com happiness is:

> 1. the quality or state of being happy.
> 2. good fortune; pleasure; contentment; joy.

Do you agree with this definition? It's not bad, is it? But there's so much more that we could add to it. Don't you think?

On a scale of 1 to 10, with 1 being not happy at all and 10 being very, very happy, how happy would you say you are right now, BEFORE reading this book?

Now remember that number. Perhaps you could write it down somewhere. Let's see if we can work together to raise it up just like a student would work to raise up his school grades.

I'm going to give you some ideas. You can take them... or leave them, but I hope you'll at least give them all a fair chance.

Without giving away my exact age, as of the time of this writing I have been on the planet for over half a century. Since I don't know you personally, I may be old enough to be your father, or young enough to be your son, but I trust you'll agree that that would be enough time to gain at least a little wisdom. Of course, you'll have to be the judge of that as you read through the book.

One of my primary goals in writing this book is to pass at least some of that wisdom on to you through the words on these pages. Please understand that I am NOT saying that I am smarter or more intelligent than you or any other person that has or will ever read this book. Just as each of the blindfolded men have information not shared by the other four, it's the same with you and me.

In fact, I want you to know upfront that although I've been on this planet for over half a century,

There is really <u>only one thing</u> I know "for sure"...

And that is...

I DON'T KNOW ANYTHING "FOR SURE"

That may sound like an amusing statement and it is, but… it is also a truthful statement. There have been times in my life when I sincerely felt that I was absolutely certain about a particular thing... and then later found out that I was either dead wrong or did not have all of the pertinent information which led to my incorrect conclusion(s). There have been times when I have misinterpreted my source, and there have been times when my source was incorrect, even though they thought they were being truthful. I suspect this may have also happened to you (or will at some point in your future). And let's not forget what I just mentioned above about our limited senses. They too may contribute to our errors in judgment.

In this book, I talk about some of my own personal experiences, but I will also be referencing things I've read in other books or heard on audio books by some of the greatest authors of our time.

But mostly it will be about things that I've noticed that I've not heard very often (if at all) that seem like common sense, yet could be very helpful if people would think about it in the same way that I do. I often find myself thinking "Am I the only one who thinks like this?" and when I point these things out to others, they are quick to agree that they make perfect sense.

I firmly believe that these things can and will help you if you will adopt them, but...

First... I Need to Gain Your Trust

If this book is really going to help you the way I intend it to, then the first thing I need to do is gain your trust.

Most of you who are reading this book will not know me, so I need to make a connection with you... I need to relate to you in some way so that you can get a sense of who I am. You will need to decide if I am a credible source, and whether or not I am worthy of your time and attention.

How Will I Do That?

The only way that I can do that is by holding your attention long enough to make some interesting points that accomplish those things. Otherwise, I will lose you and you will go on with your life and forget all about this book. And that would be a shame. I am hopeful that this will be one of those "keeper" books. You know, one that you will treasure and keep. One that you will always want to know is available to read or reread any time you want.

What I Ask of You

If you will commit to reading at least two chapters, I feel very strongly that *I will* gain your trust… that *you will* get a sense of who I am… that you will decide that I am a credible source and that at the end of this book, you will be glad that you gave me a chance to serve you.

Although I will need to make that connection by letting you gain an understanding of who I am, ***this book is <u>not</u> about me***. **It is about you**. It is about you becoming a little more faithful, a little more grateful, a little more understanding, a little more forgiving, a little more thoughtful, a little more caring, and a little more loving.

Why?

Because these are the things that beget happiness.

What I intend to do in this book is share some thoughts and ideas that could possibly help you to see things a little bit differently than you do now. And if I succeed, I'm sure you'll be as Happy as a rat in a trash can!

"Change the way you look at things and the things you look at change."

Dr. Wayne W. Dyer

———

Get wisdom, get understanding;
do not forget my words or turn away from them.
Proverbs 4: 5

Let's get started!

I hope that you have enjoyed this excerpt from Don's
"Happy As a Rat In a Trash Can"

For information about this book
Please go to Amazon.com

Disclaimer

Adherence to all applicable laws and regulations including international, federal, state and local governing professional licensing, business practices, advertising, and all other aspects of doing business in the US, Canada or any other jurisdiction is the sole responsibility of the purchaser or reader.

Neither the author nor the publisher assume any responsibility or liability whatsoever on the behalf of the purchaser or reader of these materials. Any perceived slight of any individual or organization is purely unintentional.

Made in the USA
Columbia, SC
02 January 2019